NEA
SCHOOL RESTRUCTURING SE

P9-ASG-518

Children of Promise:

Literate Activity in Linguistically and Culturally Diverse Classrooms

Shirley Brice Heath
Leslie Mangiola

Sandra R. Schecter
Glynda A. Hull
Editors

A Joint Publication of
National Education Association
Center for the Study of Writing and Literacy
American Educational Research Association

Robert M. McClure
NEA Mastery In Learning Consortium
NEA National Center for Innovation
Series Editor

nea PROFESSIONAL LIBRARY

National Education Association
Washington, DC

Printing History
   First Printing: June 1991

Note

The opinions expressed in this publication should not be construed as representing the policy or position of the National Education Association. This publication is intended as a discussion document for educators who are concerned with specialized interests of the profession.

Library of Congress Cataloging-in-Publication Data

Children of promise : literate activity in linguistically and
   culturally diverse classrooms / Shirley Brice Heath . . . [et al.].
   editors.
        p.   cm. — (NEA school restructuring series)
     "A joint publication of National Education Association, Center for
   the Study of Writing and Literacy, and American Educational Research
   Association."
     Includes bibliographical references.
     ISBN 0–8106–1844–3
     1. Literacy programs—California—Case studies.   2. Peer-group
   tutoring of students—California—Case studies.   3. Education,
   Bilingual—United States.   I. Heath, Shirley Brice.   II. National
   Education Association of the United States.   III. Center for the
   Study of Writing and Literacy.   IV. American Educational Research
   Association.   V. Series.
   LC152.C2C47   1991
   371.97—dc20   91–634
                                                                             CIP

CONTENTS

FOREWORD

Depending on your point of view about how much water is in the glass, the matter of children coming to school using languages other than English is either a problem or an opportunity. Efforts to restructure schools ought to be affected by these children and their needs. Current efforts to reshape schools to better serve all students can be vastly enriched when we build new programs that capitalize on the growing multilingualism of our students.

To capitalize on this rich resource requires educators to challenge some of their assumptions about a number of the regularities that govern our professional work. Of first order are those assumptions having to do with issues of curricular sequence and predicted rates of learning. Our practices have too often dictated rigid adherence to theories of knowledge and learning that do not stand the test of classroom reality.

Does proficiency in a second, school-dominant language always have to precede the development of concepts? Should students (whether they are English language proficient or not) always proceed from the simple to the complex in their studies?

And what of the nature of the curriculum content? Can we get better at selecting from our vast array of knowledge that which is relevant to the present and future needs of this generation? Particularly, how can the powerful role that language plays in one's education be enhanced for those who arrive at school with the gift of a language other than the one that most of us speak?

In the current efforts to improve schools we ought to be focusing attention on pedagogical issues, particularly those that can liberate and empower students. Unfortunately, *restructuring* has come to mean improving the structures of schooling—time, schedules, governance, authority. We are not getting at the heart of the matter. Conceiving and using pedagogy that has a powerful impact on students could move us from *restructuring* to *transformation.* How teachers and their communities can become more engaged in such work is a question that needs to be asked much more regularly.

In this series on school restructuring, we are attempting to strike a balance between theory and practice—indeed, building a bridge between those two, too often disparate worlds. In *Children of Promise*, the authors deal with fundamental questions about teaching and learning and curriculum. They do so in ways that represent the best of these worlds. As is so often the case in joint efforts between teachers and researchers, both are enriched.

Robert M. McClure
Series Editor

PREFACE

Children of Promise addresses one of the most important and most difficult challenges we face in American education today—improving literacy learning for *all* children, especially those who are now least well served by our nation's schools. Our future as a nation depends on ensuring that students from an increasing diversity of backgrounds achieve literacy levels far beyond the basics of reading and writing. Given rapidly changing demographics as multiple cultures meet in our schools, *Children of Promise* points us in productive directions. It results from a long-term collaboration between Leslie Mangiola, a classroom teacher, and Shirley Brice Heath, a university researcher.

Children of Promise provides a model for university-school collaboration and, fittingly, is itself the result of a complex series of collaborations between university-based researchers and school-based practitioners. The project began when the National Education Association (NEA), the largest national professional organization for teachers, and the American Educational Research Association (AERA), the largest national professional organization for educational researchers, decided to initiate a joint venture aimed at improving some aspect of American education. NEA and AERA selected the topic area of writing and literacy, and then enlisted the help of the national Center for the Study of Writing (CSW)—now the Center for the Study of Writing and Literacy—to coordinate and provide intellectual direction to the project.

As a first step, CSW brought together an advisory panel of prominent members of both NEA and AERA who had expertise in written language. These expert practitioners and researchers, along with CSW researchers, agreed unanimously on the need for collaborative thinking about the literacy needs of the culturally and linguistically diverse students who now populate our schools. The panel was concerned particularly with increasing our understanding of how to provide literacy

7

opportunities to those students who are currently least well served.

In formulating the project, the panel voted unanimously to solicit the help of Shirley Brice Heath, who was well known for her long-term collaborations with teachers who serve those students frequently pegged as the dropouts of tomorrow. The panel was particularly interested in Heath's then ongoing work with Leslie Mangiola, having heard about the successful cross-age tutoring program Heath and Mangiola had established at Fair Oaks Elementary School in Redwood City, California, where Mangiola teaches. That program trained Latina ninth graders who were failing in school to tutor young elementary students in reading. The tutors showed dramatic improvements in their own attitudes toward school and in their literacy skills. The NEA/AERA advisory panel asked Heath and Mangiola to write about their work together and, in so doing, to put forth a model for researcher-teacher collaboration. The result is *Children of Promise,* a work of immense practical and theoretical importance.

In *Children of Promise* Heath and Mangiola describe the tutoring program as well as other approaches to language learning, giving practical guidance for teachers who might want to undertake programs with similar goals. Yet their point goes beyond the "how to's." More important are their philosophy and theoretical framework, from which other educators can generate activities that can be just as successful as those described in this monograph. Their work implies that student success in formal schooling will require an educational framework that includes:

- Respecting and building on the vast language knowledge the students bring with them to school, including knowledge of languages other than English;
- Weaving language activities so that reading, writing, and oral language work together;
- Infusing the school life of the students with literacy activities that are important to them; and
- Providing the students with the help they need to

improve and perform well on literacy tasks at higher and higher levels.

Also important about *Children of Promise* is the way it developed. Heath and Mangiola found it essential to have time to work together over a number of years, without the pressures of a project with a limited time frame, and with the goal of mutual sharing and learning. They began their work deeply committed to the students' full use of two languages, and both wanted to organize the students' educational experiences so that they could have promising academic futures. Each brought expertise and resources—Heath from the university and Mangiola from her classroom experience.

The Center for the Study of Writing and Literacy has been privileged to work with Heath and Mangiola and with NEA and AERA. We all are looking for ways to improve American education and believe that if we are to quicken the pace of progress in the schools, we must bring together our multiple perspectives to solve our most difficult educational problems. *Children of Promise* invites educators to build on the collaborative work described within its pages, to invent other successful ways to teach similar children, and then to communicate these ideas to others, as Heath and Mangiola have done here. It also sets the stage for future collaborations between practitioners and researchers—collaborations that can suggest new and creative ways to improve school-based literacy learning.

Sarah Warshauer Freedman
Director
Center for the Study of Writing and Literacy

ACKNOWLEDGMENTS

Collaboration in America's public schools today comes about only if others outside the actual collaborating team also cooperate and offer their support. The authors would like to thank Gloria Norton, long-time proponent of authentic language learning opportunities for children and resource teacher at Fair Oaks Elementary School during the years of our work together. Marjorie Martus, a loyal community volunteer at elementary schools in Redwood City, modeled for us innovation and persistence in encouraging collaboration in schools. Lucinda P. Alvarez, Ronald Anderson, and Olga A. Vasquez, future educational researchers (then graduate students at the School of Education at Stanford University), also helped in innumerable ways in the cross-age tutoring. Diane Hoffman, also from Stanford's School of Education, helped edit the videofilm and guidebook that first documented this project. Currently teacher educators, these four individuals will continue to influence future teachers to allow apprenticeship and collaboration in their classrooms. We also thank James King and Kathy Riley for sharing their stories of collaboration as teacher educators who initiated university-school ties in their own regions and offered innovative additions to cross-age tutoring and student research on language learning.

Additionally, the editors would like to thank the NEA/AERA advisory panel members for their suggestions. Special thanks go to Mary Futrell and Lauren Resnick, then presidents of NEA and AERA, respectively, who initiated the collaboration. Seeing the manuscript to completion were, for AERA, president Richard Shavelson, along with his successor, Nancy Coles, and Bill Russell, executive officer; for NEA, Marcella Dianda, Ann T. McLaren, and Sharon P. Robinson; and for CSW, staff editor Andrew Bouman and editorial assistant Linda Harklau. To these colleagues, as well as to the manuscript's dedicated reviewers, we are much indebted for their generous counsel.

INTRODUCTION

We hear much talk these days of "students at risk." We hear complaints that we are ill prepared to deal with the diversity of language, culture, and background in our classrooms; predictions that students who are different culturally and linguistically, and therefore often ill served by their schooling, will be likely to fail or drop out; and warnings that such losses, with their economic and social repercussions, will seriously affect the quality of our lives in the twenty-first century. Without meaning to lessen the seriousness of such warnings—indeed, we think grave concern is warranted—we want to offer a different perspective, an obvious, but important, change in how we represent the issues at hand. In this monograph, we want to remember that the students we are becoming accustomed to labeling "at risk" are actually—like all our students—children of promise. And we want to characterize some classrooms where their promise is being realized, where teachers and students are taking care to listen, observe, and learn together.

Let us take a quick look inside one of these classrooms.

Alicia is a fifth grader with a history of poor school performance. She is also a tutor. Twice a week half her class visits a first grade classroom, while half of the first graders go to the fifth grade room. The older students like Alicia read, write, and talk with the younger ones, and then they regroup to write up their analyses of what happened during their tutoring sessions.

Following this brief time for reflection and writing, all the fifth graders join in a circle to share the problems they see in the learning of their first grade partners and to offer possible solutions. For a few minutes of their discussion, they are joined by the first graders' teacher, who listens to their assessments of the younger students' reading and writing performances and shares and compares understandings. The group comes to agree with

11

Alicia, who thinks that first graders "don't know a lot," especially about some objects, events, and places that appear in children's literature. However, Miguel suggests that his first grader "knows a lot, but he just doesn't talk about it and he won't ask me questions." Thus, the fifth graders engage in problem solving in an effort to bring the younger students to a strong confidence in their own learning abilities and an acceptance of the role of language in that learning. They want to help the first graders learn "some things," they say, but without "being boring teachers" or "just tellin''em to go look it up in a book."

In this language-minority classroom—where students speak languages or dialects other than standard English—students and teachers work closely with language researchers, asking questions about how language works in different situations for various groups of speakers and readers, and about how we all might understand and explain how language works. In this classroom, then, researchers, teachers, and students work together *to investigate language use and to prepare written materials and oral presentations about their findings for other audiences.*

In this monograph we will introduce you to a few such classrooms in more detail, describing and examining their literacy practices and setting forth some of the principles of learning and language that underlie them. In fundamental ways the teachers and students in these classrooms are engaged in the same enterprise as Miguel, Alicia, and the other fifth grade tutors—that is, they are seeking answers to questions that face us all in classrooms filled with students from diverse cultural, linguistic, and socioeconomic backgrounds: How can we enable students to use what they already know to move confidently into new learning? How can we distinguish between what our students don't know and what they just don't know how to express—in either spoken or written language?

Our search for effective, sensitive ways to empower students from diverse linguistic and cultural backgrounds to engage in meaningful learning is guided by the following credo:

Teachers, students, and researchers must be jointly active in the learning process. All must have chances to learn and to construct and revise theories about what and how they know. They must be free to use the language of give-and-take to negotiate ideas, to build knowledge, and to acquire new skills to prepare for lifelong learning.

Chapter 1

CULTURAL AND LINGUISTIC DIFFERENCES

Before entering the classrooms, let us consider some of the key social and cultural features of language-minority students' backgrounds that play a role in their responses to the expectations of formal schooling. To realize the promise of *all* our students, we educators must better understand the students' needs. In recent years we have become increasingly aware that all students do not bring the same kinds of knowledge, language habits, and strategies for learning to school, and that school is an institution that must take responsibility for presenting all students with a range of options for organizing knowledge and using language. By knowing more about the varieties of ways that language is used outside school—in community life, commercial exchanges, and service encounters—teachers and students can expand their ways of describing, clarifying, and assessing experience. These expansions of language uses in school will bring students closer to the competencies that will meet the communication needs of work opportunities and lifelong learning.

All sociocultural groups have some unique ways of transmitting to their children background knowledge about the world and of asking their children to display what they know. In some groups, adults will ask children many questions to which the adults already know the answer. Such routines may begin early and last well into early puberty: "Where's your nose?" "Can you tell Dad who we saw at the ball game tonight?" In some communities, by contrast, telling what one knows or competing overtly against another invites ridicule, censure, and even punishment from elders. Within some sociocultural groups, too,

14

adults foster opportunities for children to learn from other children, and the intervention by parents in what children learn may be minimal once the young are old enough to take care of themselves.

Some communities value highly the separation of teaching and learning, and their members speak of "raising," "bringing up," or "training" children. In other communities, such views of the power of one individual over another are replaced by concepts of "self-development" or "self-fulfillment," as children "unfold," "come up," or just "turn out to be." In the former communities, adults intervene in many actions of the young, asking children to talk about each step of procedures, to say what is already known to adults, and they elicit accounts in which children assert themselves as primary actors. Directives like "Tell me what you did today" or "Tell Aunt Mary what happened to you at school on Wednesday" place children in performing roles and allow adults to serve as spectators who can observe and monitor the learner's response to enculturation.

The point of these examples is that we all have particular expectations about learning—the appropriate ways of displaying knowledge, the roles teachers and learners can take, the information we assume is shared—and these expectations may differ sharply depending on one's culture and background. The rub comes because these expectations seem to us so "natural" that they are virtually invisible. It is difficult to penetrate such "natural" events and examine them as they might appear to children from families and communities that do not experience routinely in their everyday lives the school's ways of seeing, knowing, and telling. Certainly many teacher educators struggle to help future teachers understand what it will mean when their students do not come to school with what many textbooks and curricular materials take for granted as basic background knowledge about the world, predictable ways of displaying knowledge, and a generalized acceptance of the authority of teacher over student.

We think it crucially important, then, that educators be

vigilant to the fact that students from diverse cultural and linguistic backgrounds may bring different ways of knowing to school, different patterns of preferred interaction. Such an awareness may ease our way, reminding us that "unusual" learning performances are not so unusual after all, given an understanding of a student's background and history, and alerting us to potential disjunctures between our own and our students' often tacit expectations about language, learning, and schooling.

But let us offer a few cautions, too, lest our enthusiasm to learn about and from our students' "differences" lead us into reductive thinking. It is important, first, not to overgeneralize. We must be clear that patterns of behavior reported for students of different cultural and linguistic groups—here and elsewhere—will not occur for all members of any minority group. Within minority communities social and cultural differences can be vast. And there is variation across geographic locations and among speakers of different periods of residence within the United States and with various kinds of school experiences before coming to the United States. These observations may sound obvious, but we believe they bear repeating. Common sense certainly tells us not to expect all individuals of one race or ethnicity to behave in the same way. Yet, we sometimes accept broad and sweeping generalizations about "Hispanics," expecting certain characteristics to apply to all brown-skinned individuals who speak Spanish or have an accent identified as "Hispanic," ignoring the wide distinctions that must exist among those from different geographic regions (such as Puerto Rico, Mexico, Central America, or South America) or with varying years of settlement in the United States. In the same way, we too often assign behavioral or language characteristics to African, Chinese, or Southeast Asian groups as though each was a homogeneous whole.

A second caution has to do with an assumption about the goal of education in general that we believe is erroneous for all students, but that is especially pernicious when applied to students "at risk," students who are "different." We argue here that the what, when, and how of schooling should enable all students to break with their everyday experiences. Schooling should provide such a range of ways of seeing, knowing, thinking, and being that it will be equally challenging to all students and teachers to imagine other possibilities, take risks with learning, and transcend the boundaries of the immediacy of personal experience. Let us then not think of students of diverse backgrounds as bringing "differences" to school, but instead as offering classrooms "expansions" of background knowledge and ways of using language.

Educational institutions currently have the goal of moving people's values, skills, and knowledge toward generalized, predictable norms, and this is especially true for minority students or those for whom English is a second language. Schools now try to make all learning equally familiar, predictable, and uniformly simplified for what is often viewed as "remedial" learning. Educators tend to exaggerate certain features of group differences and to urge people to change in the direction of the mainstream or the predictable. This push to conformity often rewards those who passively accept orders, await and accept directions from others, and offer no resistance to mainstream institutions' ways of operating.

It should not be surprising that some students from all cultural groups may learn to respond as passive individuals who seem unaware, uninvolved, and disinterested in academic achievement. This is especially true if the expectations of male and female behaviors in the home and community encourage passive responses to outsiders and reward nonaggressive or unemotional displays of dissatisfaction or discomfort. Similarly, some students may come from communities or families that have encouraged individuals to respond to hardship with humor, jest, or even mock aggression.

Teaching methods and programs that stress basic literacy skills and display of knowledge in small bits of scope and in specific sequence may also reward the competition of individual against individual, rather than the sharing of group knowledge and resources with which the children of some communities have had experience in the past. Repeated requirements to compete, display as an individual, and learn without accepting responsibility for either process or the effect on peers can cut at the heart of a sense of dignity and identity for members of certain cultural groups and diminish the possibility of their achieving the school's preferred ways of displaying knowledge.

For example, in many classrooms, the spirit of group involvement and responsibility for others that Mexican-American, Black, Laotian, or Cambodian students show in their lives outside the school cannot reveal itself in positive ways. Yet, if teachers and researchers can find ways to keep that spirit active in collaborative work in the classrooms, they can not only overcome what may seem to be a resistance to learning, but also enhance the learning chances of younger students. They can also bring students whose socialization has not stressed such collaboration in learning into new sets of habits modeled by their peers of diverse backgrounds.

Alicia, as tutor of younger Lucia, could say of her expectations for the future:

> I always tell my mom that I don't want to be no schoolgirl. School girl is una, una niña que no mas se la pasa metida en sus libros [a girl who spends all her time with her head in books]. She doesn't want to go out to the dance, she doesn't want to go nowhere because she just wants to do her homework.

Her friends offered support for this idea:

> To know your math—that means that you're a schoolgirl.

> A schoolgirl is a dumb thing.

For individuals to acquire and to display knowledge just from books is unacceptable to Alicia. To bring the knowledge of books to bear on dynamic and generative activities—such as tutoring, writing social studies texts for younger students, and preparing scripts for a school radio broadcast—is acceptable. The basis of such knowledge is a reliance on the expertise of the learner in some domain or activity. This is in essence what the otherwise dissimilar classrooms located in different geographic areas that we are about to visit have in common.

Chapter 2

INSIDE CLASSROOMS

LEARNING THROUGH CROSS-AGE, INTERACTIVE TUTORING: CALIFORNIA

Fair Oaks Elementary School in Redwood City, California, with more than 90 percent of its student population non-native English speakers, began in the early 1980s to stress wide-ranging spoken and written language uses (from a student radio program to student publications) in a whole-language approach. Teachers and administrators worked with a reading/ language arts curriculum based on children's literature and a conception of the connectedness of spoken and written language across the curriculum. Both students and teachers participated in discussions of ways to build new methods and materials into the language-based learning approach of the bilingual school. In 1983 they decided to add cross-grade, interactive tutoring to their school's numerous language activities.

Several teachers and university researchers developed plans for a pull-out program for teacher-identified, "at-risk" fifth graders in the first year. This program was simply a short first step; the real goal was to involve whole classes and incorporate cross-grade tutoring in several classrooms. However, the pull-out program, as a brief pilot, helped provide pointers and gave the school the chance to collect a large library of Spanish and English books for the use of the tutors in all the classrooms.

In the pilot, teachers volunteered to allow certain students needing reading improvement—initially ten Mexican-American girls—to work with the four program directors and twenty tutees on reading twice a week for an hour and a half. During a two-week orientation period the program directors

20

modeled story reading, emphasizing such things as varying intonation to capture the listener's interest and asking questions of many different types (e.g., comprehension questions, prediction questions), and suggested that students engage in discussion about related personal experiences. Accounting for what was happening in the tutoring sessions was also strongly emphasized; tutors were instructed to take field notes after the day's tutoring session was finished, to view and analyze their videotapes, to interview their tutees, and to report to the first graders' teachers. Field notes were used to assess the tutors' as well as the tutees' progress.

During the tutoring sessions students were video- and audiotaped. Program directors also observed the sessions and took notes on what was happening. After the reading sessions, researchers met with the tutors in small groups to talk about their tutoring. The tutors were encouraged to talk about what they themselves did as readers and writers, and about what they did with their tutees in order to keep interest and to encourage reading. Here are some questions that were commonly discussed:

- What kinds of questions did the tutees ask?
- What books did they choose?
- How did they like the books?
- What changes have you observed in the tutees' behavior?
- What new ways might be used to challenge the tutees to move on to more difficult books?
- How does your tutee's response to books compare with your memory of your early experiences with books?

The goal of these discussions was to help tutors see themselves as becoming "experts" about the processes of reading, writing, and talking about what can be learned from personal experience, books, and the oral retellings of others.

The following description (taken from the tutors' book about tutoring) was written by a tutor and lists what she felt her responsibilities were:

1. Help kids to get a book.
2. Ask them questions about the books.
3. Tell them not to play.
4. Help them read.
5. Help them finish their words.
6. Ask them if they liked the pictures.
7. Ask them what page they liked more.
8. Say good things to the tutees. For example, when they answer a question, you say, "That is very good."
9. Let them pick their own book.
10. Show them how to read. For example, read the word first, then let them say it after you.
11. Tell them not to talk.
12. Tell them to listen.
13. Encourage them to talk about the book. Ask the kids to imagine if something like in the book happened to you.
14. Save your notes.
15. Have the children sit by you.
16. Show them the book's pictures.
17. Ask prediction questions.
18. Answer the kid's questions.
19. Let them read wordless books.
20. Help them on their spelling.
21. Show them their ABC's.
22. Help them sound words.
23. Let them draw about the book.
24. Let them ask you what the word means.
25. Let the kids read whenever they want.

One important aspect of this project was that tutors and tutees could read and interact in the language they felt most comfortable using. Whether the tutors read in Spanish or English, they asked the same sorts of questions and made the same progress in their writing and literate behaviors. This is because acquiring the ability to talk about reading and writing is not dependent on the particular language used or on the particular learning context. Rather, the ability to talk and think "literately" is a fundamental skill that is transferable to all areas of academic performance.

Having a younger audience to interact with gives student tutors a chance to see themselves as sources of knowledge that matter to someone other than a distant adult. Tutors learn what kinds of questions to ask, how to involve their listeners in reading and talking, and how to evaluate their own as well as their tutees' reactions to the texts. When given a chance to act as responsible persons capable of guiding younger readers, tutors become engaged not only in reading, but also in reflective activities, such as writing field notes, which allow them to assess their own and their tutees' progress. When tutors can step back and reflect about what they and their tutees are doing, they begin to acquire fundamental characteristics of literate behaviors.

What were the results of the project? Why did other teachers in the school begin to adopt aspects of interactive reading and writing for their students?

1. Over time, students who began the program speaking and reading exclusively in Spanish began to read and discuss books with their tutees in English. This shift illustrates the transfer of literate behaviors independent of specific language context.
2. Though the goal of the project was not simply to make the tutors "feel good" or to give them added self-confidence, their classroom teachers noticed a growth in their willingness to speak out in class and to take leadership roles.
3. Overall there was a greater tendency later in the project for tutors to vary their intonation in reading, to ask different types of questions, and to relate books to personal experience. However, many tutors consistently stayed close to basic, comprehension-level questions, such as "¿Qué es eso?" ("What is that?") Often they were more interested in whether or not their tutees could answer a question with a short, "correct" answer than in whether the text had meaning and value for their young listeners.
4. Toward the end of the project the tutors increasingly steered their tutees to use positive books, to try sounding out words, to retell stories using puppets, and to write stories. These

changes occurred as tutors realized what they could do to get their listeners more involved in reading. In sum, they became aware of both their tutees' uses of language and of language as a source of data for reporting on learning.

5. Tutors began to appreciate the literate development of their tutees, as seen in comments in letters to the tutees and their teachers at the end of the year, comments that expressed "happiness" about the tutees' attempts at writing and reading. One tutor, for example, mentioned how glad she was that her tutee could read so many words. This pride in development may signal an emerging awareness of the value of being literate and successful in school.

Following the pilot pull-out program, several classes adopted cross-grade, interactive tutoring. In this plan, fifth or sixth graders and kindergartners or first graders split their classes twice each week for approximately thirty minutes. One-half of an upper grade class switched places with one-half of a lower grade class for the tutoring period. After the tutoring, the older students wrote field notes about what had happened during the tutoring period and then shared in an open class meeting their particular problems, successes, or new strategies and plans for their next tutorial session. Teachers also observed and brought their questions to the group: "Tammy, I noticed your tutee was very restless today, and you seemed to quiet him down so easily. Could you share with the rest of us how you accomplished that?"

Such occasions allowed teachers to ask of their students certain questions that they might usually expect to ask only of their teacher colleagues: "How would you present this book to a particularly shy tutee or an unwilling reader?" "How could you encourage your tutee to try new kinds of books?" One teacher chose to explain readability formulas to her class as a mathematics exercise, and in so doing, she asked students' views of the formulas for their work with their tutees. Interest sharpened considerably when this previously abstract mathematics problem related to their own roles as critics. Students raised serious questions about how the formulas worked and whether or not a particular readability score had anything to say about "good stories." The class then read together Carl Sandburg's poem "Fog," discussing whether or not first graders in their region might understand the simple words, but complex images of the poem. Their conclusion was that the answer depended on what "little kids bring to the text—what they know before they read about what they're going to read."

Why would teachers try this kind of interactive reading and writing? How do such activities differ from programs that pair older and younger students simply for tutoring and do not integrate the language and learning analysis of the tutoring sessions into the curriculum?

1. Teachers in cross-grade tutoring projects spend less time disciplining children and more time in individual consultation. Tutoring frees teachers from the need to maintain a single focus of attention in a class, a task that is often draining and eventually boring.

2. Cross-grade tutoring provides numerous authentic occasions for extensive and highly motivated student writing. "Dead-end" writing assignments whose only audience is the teacher become far more infrequent (and are often eliminated entirely) and are replaced with writing tasks that engage students in real communication with an audience. Creating more opportunities for children to write naturally in the course of their reading can lead to frequent, natural, and extensive writing.

3. Field notes, letters to tutees or teachers, book synopses, and student profiles are types of extended writing that students engage in voluntarily once they become committed to their role as sources of knowledge and models of skills for the younger students.

4. Tutoring gives teachers a chance to step out of their usual roles as "directors" to fulfill roles as "facilitators" who are in much greater contact with students as learners and who

146, 344

25

therefore can more easily help students build on their own experiences and background knowledge.

Appendix A contains detailed suggestions for implementing a cross-grade tutoring program.

OBSERVING AND WRITING ABOUT TEACHING AND LEARNING: TEXAS

In an elementary school in Texas, fifth and sixth grade students involved in a similar interactive tutoring program decided to write a booklet for parents based on their experiences helping younger children to read and write. Here is how this booklet came about.

James King, a professor at Texas Woman's University, was working in cooperation with staff from a nearby elementary school to develop a plan whereby university students from his child development classes would work with parents from a community with a low-achieving elementary school. The idea was to help these parents learn to feel comfortable in reading with their children at home. Students agreed, school staff cooperated, announcements went out, and no parents showed up.

King quickly recognized the imposing role that he and his university students had tried to assume over the parents they wanted to support. A revised plan involved fifth and sixth graders, all low achievers, in reading activities with kindergartners. Initially, King and his students took field notes and videotaped the reading sessions. Gradually, however, the visitors moved into the background, just like sixth grader Mark recommended: "We can do it; we can observe and record what the little kids are doing when they read. We don't need you to do it." And, thus, the sixth graders began observing as well as reading with the younger children, alternating days on which they undertook each type of task. Students kept records of the kinds of books they read, their lengths, and the responses of the younger children.

Once involved in the tutoring and observing, the students saw the need for other changes in Professor King's plans: They rearranged furniture, displayed books, and organized rotating schedules so that at least three readers could be videotaped each day. Sharing permeated their time together; they saw no reason not to share everything: books, reading spots, responsibilities, tape recorders, turns, permissions, and calls for courtesy.

The tutors made the following observations about the kindergartners (whom they referred to as the "K's") in their field notes:

- Being in charge when sharing a book is important.
- Have manners for other readers.
- Let K's pick out books too.
- Listeners look at the books, pay attention, and sit still when they are interested.
- You can keep the K's attention by the way you hold the book, talk about the story, and who turns the pages.

They drew these conclusions about "good readers":

- Good readers emphasize the words and put expression and feeling into their reading.
- Good readers get the words, but it's OK to make up words when you don't know or the K is drifting off.
- Good readers don't go too fast or too slow.
- Good readers ask questions about what will happen next, what pictures mean, and if the K liked the story.

These students decided to share what they had learned about reading with kindergartners in a booklet they prepared for parents of incoming first graders. Here they offered assessments of the difficulties of reading with young children and gave helpful hints for parents willing to undertake the challenge. The following excerpts from the introduction to their book reveal the serious learning these fifth and sixth graders achieved through this experience:

We are fifth and sixth graders and we've studied kindergartners. We read to them and also watched how they act when you read to them. When we started the program, we listened to Mr. King read stories. He told us what to do and read to us to get the idea. When we read to the kindergartners, they were nervous, but not us. Dave said he was scared, but he read.

So we started reading to the kindergartners. Then we started videotaping the readers while they read to the children. We also tape-recorded our reading and listened to the tapes. We watched the videos of our reading to see what we had read to the kids.

We also had the kids draw pictures from the book when we finished reading. The kids drew pictures about the books and sometimes we wrote on it for them.

After reading to the kids for several weeks, we started taking notes. One group read to the kids and the other group took notes on what the reader was doing. Mr. King gave us notepads to take notes on all the readers. We took notes as we watched the motions of the readers and the children and wrote down what we saw. We also wrote about what other notetakers were doing.

With all of these different things going on, our room got pretty confusing at times. We saw that commotion gets in the way. Kindergartners couldn't get involved with the book. They looked away at the noises and talking. They do look back at the book but only after it quiets down.

Kindergartners move around a lot. It is hard for some of them to sit still. Even when they are interested in the story, they twitch their hands and feet.

We also saw that picking out a book is not easy. Sometimes we picked out the books. When the kids picked the books, sometimes they wanted the same book over and over. We couldn't tell which kids would like which books. It changed with different kids. Some like comedy, funny characters and pictures. When we talked with the kids, we could usually tell which books they would like. We're still not sure why some kids like one book over others. One of the readers thinks it's because the kid has already heard the book. The kindergartners seem to like the books they know.

We discovered that some kindergartners know words and want to read along when they can. Others can read a page back after we read it to them. Some other kids memorized books and acted like they were reading the words.

Another thing we learned is how hard it is to read to two kids at once. When we tried to do this, the kids would both want their book read first. We had to pick one of the books. The kid who didn't get their book read would not pay attention at first. It was a lot easier to read to one kindergartner at a time.

After all this project, we have some ideas to share about reading to kids.

Their book follows with general recommendations about the merits of reading, where to read, how to read, how to pick books, how to talk and ask questions, and "some other things"—a section that included this comment:

Above all, there are some *nevers*. Never lose your temper over reading. Just stop and do something else. Never make a kid read. They may not be able to.

They ended the book with brief summaries and assessments they had made of some of the kindergartners' favorite books.

The achievements for students in this project included reduced truancy and discipline problems, extended opportunities for integrating language arts activities, and a heightened awareness of the teacher's and learners' respective responsibilities. Moreover, through repetitive voluntary engagement with producing, editing, revising, and publishing expository and narrative texts in Standard English, learners developed an appreciation for the power of the written word and the motivation to use it as a tool of empowerment.

COLLECTING AND ANALYZING SPOKEN AND WRITTEN LANGUAGE DATA: MASSACHUSETTS

In the previous example of language-based learning, students took classroom language experiences and used them to inform the community. In another classroom in Boston,

Massachusetts, adult students used the language of the community to inform their class curriculum.

Kathy Riley, of Roxbury Community College in Boston, Massachusetts, worked with her second-year English-as-a-second-language conversation class to collect and analyze language data. Briefed on the class goals before enrolling, her students—representing eleven different language communities—spent the first semester audiotaping oral language; during the second term, they focused on written language. They took part as well in some collaborative work with an outside language researcher (Shirley Brice Heath), who had met with the students on their first day of class and promised to serve as a technical consultant and to join the class as an inquiring language learner—corresponding with them via mail and returning to their classroom every eight weeks or so throughout the year.

The first week of school the students carried out informal observations in their homes, on their jobs, and in the streets. They brought the language data they collected back to class, discussed the chaos, shared the frustration, and worked out a simple observation instrument that would standardize their future data collection efforts. For example, they agreed on the need to "write exactly the same words that are spoken." They also acknowledged the need to identify speakers, mark turns among them, and take into account the specific situation in which talk occurred by writing brief descriptions of setting and context. By mid-October, the group had collected, analyzed, and written up explanations of six observations. The students had also composed and sent a letter off to Heath explaining what they had done. By the end of the semester, they had studied the following types of oral language uses: casual service encounters (bank transactions, asking street directions, etc.); oral work assignments in job settings; comparisons of television broadcasts, radio reports, and first paragraphs of newspaper reports of the same event; the simplified language of Saturday morning cartoons; foreigner talk; and talk to young children. The next semester they applied similar methods to the study of different types of written

30

language. For example, they listed the features of "scientific" writing, including the use of numerous causal connectors, such as *because, therefore,* and *as a result.* They compared types of public writing—from public health brochures to political campaign leaflets—and identified features of persuasive language, techniques of linking pictures with text, and manipulative language. They studied the language of instructions—in laboratory manuals, practice materials for standardized tests, and end-of-chapter review units of textbooks. They experimented with rewriting these instructions.

What did these students learn as a result of this unorthodox English curriculum? Consider these language-based activities:

1. In the first weeks of their observations, the students initiated discussion and requests for explication of several points in grammar: the deletion of -*s* as a marker of third-person singular present tense. the deletion of past tense markers such as -*ed*; and the simplification of verbs using the auxiliary *to be* (e.g., *he working*).

2. They moved on to a discussion of how English seems to have many ways of "saying the same thing" and voiced their concerns about the use of Black dialect. They also considered the differences between dialects of Spanish in the United States and in Latin America.

3. They asked their teacher for information about the ways in which vocabulary becomes specialized by age, vocation, sport, and sociocultural group.

4. They recognized the need to develop terms to describe styles of language—from colloquial to formal. They noted differences in vocabulary and syntax between informal conversations on certain topics and news coverage of the same topic, for example, an athletic event. Terms such as "research," "data," "evidence," "counter-example," "dialect," and "turn-taking" became part of their daily vocabulary.

By the end of the term the students' transcriptions of their own data had become so expert, and their methods of analysis so keen, that they could determine subtle sentence structure differences between native speakers and non-native speakers and differentiate "real" conversations from invented ones or literary dialogue. But, more than this, by explicitly studying language use in their surrounding community, learners became more attentive to their own uses of language and how they might use language more effectively to get things done.

Listen to what these students had to say of their learning:

I listen now. I can't hear a native English speaker without having some understanding of what is going on and why.

I learn a lot of good spelling words and some English rules.

I know that I am going to learn faster, because I have better opportunities to socialize and communicate with others who are in business and [the] highest positions. I have confidence in this course and myself because the process and the analysis that we are following are excellent, and our group work[s] very hard to help each other.

These quotations from Kathy Riley's non-native English-speaking students suggest learners who are not only engaged, but also taking charge of their own literate behaviors. Their words also hint at the complex and multiple ways in which those learners who are not part of "mainstream" society and/or who have traditionally been regarded as "at risk" have learned *both language and about language* in a class designed to help them recognize the role of language in learning.

Chapter 3

WRITING, LEARNING, AND THE TEACHER'S ROLE

VIEWING LANGUAGE AS AN INSTRUMENT AND OBJECT OF STUDY

So far we have looked inside three classrooms and observed students, teachers, and researchers listening, observing, and learning from one another. The students were learners thought to need some sort of special language treatment, and all were in classes with teachers or supplementary instructional personnel who chose to regard themselves and their students as language researchers or inquirers. Teachers and students came to view themselves as in-charge learners who could ask questions about their own language and that of others, assess their own learning progress, and influence the direction of their learning retention and extension by taking the skills they acquired in the classroom into their jobs, business transactions, and leisure activities.

The language-based learning that went on in these classrooms had two practices in common:

1. Teachers asked students to record—sometimes by audiotaping and sometimes by taking field notes—their language habits and those of their primary networks (i.e., friends and families) and secondary networks (i.e., employment, commercial, and social voluntary associations). With teachers' permission, some students recorded classroom language, analyzing interactions and interviewing teachers and students about their reflections on what happens in classroom talk. Similarly, some students tape-recorded and analyzed their own group work or tutoring sessions.

33

2. Teachers and students used the language data for discussions that led to expository reports on patterns in talk and written text. As students analyzed the collections of language for which they were the experts (only they could tell the teacher who the speakers were and what transpired as a result of the communication), they began to see how language works as an instrument of social interaction.

What characterizes the language learning of the *students* in the classrooms described here? What makes these activities carry more potential for student retention and extension of language skills—greater potential, we would argue, than writing pen-pal letters, interviewing grandparents for a social studies lesson, or preparing a class newspaper? At the heart of this learning is a sustained dual-track approach: a focus on *language as both instrument and object of study.* In these classrooms everyone caught on to the fact that oral and written language is central to accomplishing the tasks at hand. Hence, students *and* teachers in these classes observed and tracked, recorded and reported on, explored and reflected on, acted on and interacted with oral and written language, accounting for not only what happens with a text, but also *how* it happens.

What characterizes the learning of the *teachers* described here? What makes their practices differ from those who have in the past taken up the inquiry approach or offered discovery units? In these classrooms teachers are learners whose major role shifts from that of cajoler (who pushes and promotes higher motivations, more practice, and greater self-confidence for students) to that of collaborator, recorder, and technical expert. Notebook or tape recorder always in hand, these teachers keep track of what is happening and report these events back to students, asking for their interpretations, seeking ideas for change, and tabulating the specifics of language learning.

If, for example, specific problems keep reappearing in students' oral or written texts, teachers report them, initiating discussion on how often and where they occur, and enabling students to analyze how they came to be. Similarly, as individual students begin to master certain language forms or uses, these merit what may be termed "positive learning" lessons, brief occasions for calling attention to the specific skills and strategies that the learner has accomplished, with ample editorial comment by the learner as expert. Moreover, through the approaches to language and learning described here, teachers learn much about the daily lives of their students outside of school.

Teachers who ask students to collect language data beyond the classroom must, of course, take responsibility for providing guidelines about the material appropriate for recording and reporting back to classmates. Private family interactions, sacred religious rites, and gossip exchanges with peers are not suitable material, first of all, because they invade students' intimate lives. Part of the experience for students in learning to be a researcher is learning to be responsible about the selection and reporting of data so as to protect the intimate and private communicative habits of families and individuals. Such language materials are inappropriate for classroom use also because they do not carry the potential for analysis and transfer that nonintimate or public language uses do. On the other hand, students can collect data on talk leading up to an athletic event; exchanges between clerk and client in transactions at service stations, banks, and grocery stores; talk about radio or television shows; and debate at open community meetings. It is in part the failure to use public language according to "mainstream" standards that holds students back from academic and vocational success; such public language—oral and written—should therefore be the focus of classroom language analysis.

The teachers described here—and others who have taken part in similar interactive language study with students of various linguistic and cultural backgrounds—are constant theory builders, forming analogies across learning situations, transforming and translating findings, predicting and questioning. They have generated independently many hypotheses about first and second language acquisition, and their theoretical conclusions regarding language socialization provide the underpinnings of their daily operations.

FINDING EXPERTISE IN THE LEARNER

To help ensure lifelong learning we can start from an initial premise: Across individuals, as well as across cultures, the learner possesses a range of bodies of expertise, and it is on this expertise that learning from books and responding to texts and tests will build. Finding these bodies of expertise is not easy and requires imagination on the part of teachers and researchers. With language, however, the task is somewhat easier than it is with chemistry, physics, or even social studies. All neurologically sound individuals are already experts at using language, observing the world about them, and finding ways to protect their egos. What researchers and teachers have to do is tap into these abilities to intensify students' commitment to learning from sources (both written and oral) beyond their direct experiences and to sharing this learning in acceptable ways.

All students must learn to write and speak about what they know to unknowing and, occasionally, even resistant audiences. Fifth grade tutor Ruben expresses his frustration with the resistance of the younger learner it is his responsibility to tutor with a sense of realism:

> Sometimes a tutee doesn't want to read, and I ask him if he want to write. He doesn't want to do that, either. Last time, my tutee said that he wanted someone else to read to him, so I said I was going to have somebody else read to him. My tutee then felt bad and said, "O.K. I want you to read to me." Sometimes you get problems and you don't get to solve them—like Tony. He had a problem and he couldn't solve it. That's why he had to change tutees.

The goal of the several kinds of learning noted in this monograph is to build on and add to the skills and values of all students and to bring them into situations where they can be used to meet academic expectations and requirements. Our intention here is not to urge teachers to teach in special ways to students whose everyday cultural and linguistic habits differ from those of the classroom. Instead, we want to urge teachers to make schooling equally strange for all students and thus to expand the ways of thinking, knowing, and expressing knowledge of all students through incorporating many cultural tendencies.

USING LANGUAGE FOR IDENTIFYING AND SOLVING PROBLEMS

Much of everyday language centers around identifying problems and then figuring out ways either to solve or to get around them. In classrooms—in contrast to the world beyond—teachers, texts, and tests provide students with problems to be solved; rare are the opportunities for students to identify problems, state them in comprehensible terms, and consider alternative solutions or bypasses. Kathy Riley, whose English-as-a-second language class we described above, asked her intermediate students to identify problems of communication in work settings (exchanges in which bosses gave directions, for example) and in service encounters (situations that involved asking directions, cashing checks, ordering at a restaurant, etc.). In class, students grouped themselves according to the situations they had studied. They then considered the following sorts of issues: (1) how they identified the problem in the situation, (2) how speakers either avoided solving the problem or tried to negotiate a solution, and (3) whether or not any general trends appeared across either work settings or service encounters.

In these group sessions students talked about the language they had observed and recorded. For example, they considered ways of asking for clarification and discussed how such requests differed across cultures and individuals of different genders and ages. They also later listened to the tape recordings of their own attempts to identify the particular problems of miscommunication from the evidence they had collected outside the classroom.

Replicating these conditions in schooling, as a way of promoting thinking, talking, analyzing, and reflecting on communication, can provide all students with some needed opportunities to contribute to the general pool of knowledge in the classroom. Consider the following scenario. A teacher wants his or her students to bring their real-world knowledge about how to identify and solve problems—especially those of human relations—to bear on their reading of literature. Thus, before students read a literary work, they are asked to record or take notes on interactions in which any of the following occurred: what was not said was the most important part of a conversation; individuals showed off their power through language; someone tried to describe a strong emotion to an inattentive listener. These student-generated texts serve as the basis for considerable talk about the specific problem in the interaction. Students then move on to read short stories that revolve around one or several of the kinds of texts that students have captured from real life.

Notice that this practice is the reverse of the more usual procedure of having students *first* read literature and *then* compare their own experiences with those in texts. Collecting and analyzing texts occurring in real space and time can help students develop a sense of expertise from their own experiences that will give them confidence and an identifiable base of everyday knowledge to refer to later in discussing literary works.

One idea in group work is for each group in the class to work on a different focus so that every group can then inform the others of some new information. Students thus have authentic reasons for expecting their answers to carry some significance for the class as a whole. Students need to be in a position to tell the class something no other group knows or may have considered. In short, the more oral opportunities students have to explain to others the language material they have collected and the interpretations and comparisons they have made, the more readily they will develop the facility for judging the sorts of background information they must include in written explanations. This kind of motivation is especially important for language-minority students who may have had relatively few opportunities in classrooms to feel that their real-world experiences bear much relationship to the formal curriculum.

Chapter 4

LITERATE BEHAVIORS BUILD LITERACY SKILLS

DEFINING LITERATE BEHAVIORS

We want to argue that teaching reading and writing by requiring that students first understand the "basics of literacy skills" before they move on to "higher-order skills" turns the natural process of language learning upside down. Young children learning to speak their mother tongue do not learn initial sounds before simple words, or simple sentences before the expression of complex emotions or desires. Instead, they first need or want; then they communicate. So it is that very young children express themselves through intonation, nonverbal gestures, and combined sounds. Rather than learning one sound or word at a time, they honor the larger purposes of their communication: conveying desire or pain, showing recognition, or sharing an experience from their past. Only after they have mastered these very complex ways of using language do they come to focus on getting specific sounds, words, or sentence structures right according to the norms of adults.

Literacy skills, as they are most often defined in the context of schooling, are mechanistic abilities that focus on separating out and manipulating discrete elements of a text—such as spelling, vocabulary, grammar, topic sentences, and outlines—outside the text as a whole. We want to underscore, however, the distinction between such literacy skills and what we consider to be literate behaviors. Although both kinds of literacies are acquired through schooling, only literate behaviors enable students to communicate their analyses and interpretations through extended text—the type of language that lies at the heart of academic study. Literate behaviors are ways of going about learning that treat language as both the medium and the

40

object of study. These behaviors that are key to academic literacy include the ability to provide sequenced explanations, logical arguments, grounded interpretations, and abstract analyses. Aside from their role in cognition, these behaviors also form the basis for social interaction in classrooms. Moreover, literate behaviors in school can be independent of any particular academic subject. Though most often thought of in terms of language arts, they underlie success in any academic area.

PROMOTING LITERATE BEHAVIORS

Pedagogical approaches that promote these academic literate behaviors rest on the assertion that we cannot expect students to be able to write about what they are reading and thinking unless they can first talk through their ideas and information. Becoming academically literate means, then, more than acquiring the "mechanics" of writing and reading; it means learning to

- interpret texts,
- say what they "mean,"
- tie them into personal experience,
- link them with other texts,
- explain and argue with passages of text,
- make predications based on the text,
- hypothesize outcomes or related situations,
- compare and evaluate, and
- talk about doing all of the above.

Many educators have the gut-level feeling that they should give more attention to oral language in classrooms to promote improved academic abilities, but they worry about ways to assess development or to identify features that mark improvement. Numerous teachers believe that a wide range of opportunities to sustain talk with others on a single topic is one of the most effective ways of building effective writing and

41

reading. These teachers have therefore had to find ways to document their students' oral language growth and to link particular kinds of changes in oral language with improvements in students' abilities to express themselves in different types of written texts (e.g., explanations or descriptions).

Perhaps the most efficient method is to rely on occasional audiotapings of in-class discussion groups. Early in the term, when the class breaks into groups for discussion, the teacher asks each group to audiotape its talk. The next day each group does a rough transcription from the tape of its talk considering how the group's sharing of conversational turns worked. Several such transcripts may be necessary before students begin to develop a knack for identifying speakers at different turns and separating the transcripts into different kinds of talk. But from the study of such transcripts, classes can begin to point to different features of successful problem-identifying and problem-solving talk. They can then list these features and consider why they see them as important in helping the group achieve its task in the group talk. Students of ten or eleven can make such transcriptions and bring astute observations to their assessments of conversations in which they have participated.

Students in several such classes have developed a "Think Talk" coding sheet in order to begin to characterize successful conversations. Students defined successful conversations as those during which speakers were engaged with and knowledgeable about the topic of the conversation, considerate of other speakers, and capable of both expressing their own thoughts clearly and building from the ideas of others.

It is critical to note that the features of successful conversations identified by the students both draw from and cut across characteristics that members of different cultural groups or genders may bring to school. The features listed on the coding sheets that follow are those the students judged to be most effective in public and institutional settings. The characteristics are listed just as the students stated them and reflect their common-sense descriptions of conversational talk-on-task.

42

Exhibit 1
Coding Sheet from an Intermediate English-as-a-Second-Language Class in High School

Each time you hear one of the following on the tape, place a check mark under the speaker's name. For #6, give one check for a, two for b, and three for c.

Student names: Angelica   Lucia   Marco   Kim

1. Successful interruption or break into talk of someone who speaks too long   _____   _____   _____   _____

2. Asking a question (this includes saying "I don't know; can you tell me?")   _____   _____   _____   _____

3. Correcting an error in English quickly—without many "uh, uh's"   _____   _____   _____   _____

4. Building what you say from what someone else in the group has said   _____   _____   _____   _____

5. Helping someone else get a turn to talk ("What do you think, Lee?")   _____   _____   _____   _____

6. Asking for clarification

   a. "Huh?" "What?"   _____   _____   _____   _____
   b. "Would you say that again?"   _____   _____   _____   _____
   c. "Do you mean [+ paraphrase of what was said]?"   _____   _____   _____   _____

7. Referring to the source of information [= telling where an idea came from]   _____   _____   _____   _____

Exhibit 2
Coding Sheet from a Basic English/Remedial Writing Class in Middle School

Student names:	Margo	Tony	Lee	Christie
1. Calling attention to the difference between what someone said and what he/she meant	___	___	___	___
2. Basing a statement on some written source	___	___	___	___
3. Using an if-then statement ("But if we accept that, then. . . .")	___	___	___	___
4. Encouraging someone else to express his/her ideas or add information	___	___	___	___
5. Asking for or offering a definition of a word or concept	___	___	___	___
6. Keeping the talk on topic ("But back to the question we started with. . . .")	___	___	___	___
7. Making a comment about the merits of a particular way of saying something ("I really like the way Mark said that—let's write that down.")	___	___	___	___
8. Asking someone to repeat an idea to make it clearer	___	___	___	___

STUDENTS AND TEACHERS AS CO-EVALUATORS

Teachers who have asked their students to become involved in keeping records of their language development in the ways we have illustrated in this monograph find that mechanical errors slip away over a relatively short period of time. As Nancie Atwell has proposed, teachers can identify particular recurring difficulties in students' oral and written language and target these for mini-lessons. Authentic occasions for talking, writing, and thinking about *effectiveness and correctness* in communication provide intense and meaningful practice with different language forms.

Students from classes that have studied the use of language in problem solving have sometimes proposed that some portion of their final grades assess their oral performance in group work sessions. To supplement standardized tests, teachers and students have explored various ways to create in portfolios some permanent records of students' spoken and written language. For example, throughout the term students keep in portfolios all their writing and a log of selected types of oral language performances (class reports, group discussions, interviews, etc.). Near the end of the term students choose five or six pieces of writing that they see as reflecting the ways they have used *writing to learn* during the term. Students might choose a particular set of class notes, penciled outlines for a project, an essay answer from an examination, or a single essay or section of a research paper. They write a brief analysis or series of explanations of how writing these pieces contributed to their learning; they characterize the strengths and weaknesses of each, along with some reference to the conditions of writing various pieces. They can do the same for types of reading they have done over the term.

In addition, they include some oral performances in their portfolio by providing a series of coding sheets of group discussions—with some analysis of changes in their oral language proficiency over the course of the term. They may also offer a brief analysis of a particular section of a tape-recorded oral report or of an editing conference with another student in a writing group. Students sometimes find that some of the features they identify most frequently as successful in group conversations also begin to appear in their written expositions: transitions, restated references to the topic, examples from written sources, statements that acknowledge multiple causes, building one's own idea in connection with the ideas of others, and so on.

When teachers feel the need during the term to track what is happening in group discussions, they take home at regular intervals a fifteen-minute audiotape of different students engaged in small-group class discussions. The teacher might play the tape in the car on the drive home and then replay the tape once in the evening and code (using a student-developed coding sheet similar to those illustrated above) the individual turns of each of the three or four participants in the group. After coding a group discussion, the teacher posts the score sheet and returns the tape to a master file; students are encouraged to double check the score sheet by listening to the tape and re-evaluating the record made by the teacher. If the class size is approximately thirty students, each student's language can be coded at least once every six weeks. At the end of the term the teacher can compare early and later code sheets for individual students in order to obtain a sense of change across time.

THE PURPOSE OF STUDENT INVOLVEMENT IN ASSESSMENT

Assessment that is authentic must actively engage students so that they understand not only what they know, but also how they can learn more and do so more effectively. To experience successful interactive reading and writing activities of the sort that characterized language learning at Fair Oaks Elementary School, in the Texas school, and at Roxbury Community College, both students and teachers need to be involved in the analysis of student writing and reading. They must therefore take part in a very different kind of "assessment" than that represented by standardized tests, which call for "short answers" such as multiple choice and sentence completions and allow for little or no room to interpret or relate text to personal experience.

In the three classrooms we have just looked into, teachers and students themselves become evaluators who are concerned not only with what they know, but also with how they communicate this knowledge in reading and writing interactions with others. This kind of knowledge means thinking about communication in a way that goes beyond issues of mechanics to larger issues of effectiveness. Cohesion within paragraphs, coherence across paragraphs, clarity of expression at the sentence level, and precision in word choice mark these larger concerns.

One primary goal in involving students in the collection, analysis, and assessment of their language is to enable them to see themselves as *experts over their own communication abilities.* They have responsibility for asking and answering questions regarding evidence they have created and about which they have considerable knowledge. They can examine the effectiveness of their expression in talk through questions of the following sort:

- What qualities of your writing (or speaking) reflected in the samples you have chosen do you consider most effective for the purposes of the communication?
- Who are the audiences of the pieces you have chosen?
- Can you remember anything about the amount of time you spent thinking about the writing before putting pen to paper for the pieces you have chosen?
- How did you prepare for the oral language pieces you have chosen?
- Which one would you like to keep in a scrapbook or as a recording for your children to see or hear someday?

Chapter 5

BUILDING THEORY AND PRACTICE TOGETHER

What do the strategies of the students and teachers we have presented in this monograph mean for the ever-expanding language-minority populations of North American schools? Do the kinds of language-learning situations described here truly hold promise for those students at greatest risk? And what do we mean by promise?

Outside the narrow confines of academic goals and school testing, what we mean by *promise* is potential entry into the job market and the functional performance of daily transactions in a heavily bureaucratized society. Individuals need to be able to support their families economically and socially, and the better their psychological well-being, the better they can accomplish these goals. Over the past ten years, as schools have increasingly turned to the tracking of minute skills, the testing of minimal competencies, and a dependency on scope-and-sequence learning tied to school textbooks and workbooks, other institutions in society have been rapidly moving in the opposite direction.

American businesses in the mid-1970s began to look hard at their own institutions, to assess their past practices for promoting productivity, and to compare philosophies underlying the incentives for their own employees with those provided in Japan and other highly successful industrial nations. The need for workers to be able to solve problems, explicate them, and negotiate and collaborate with their colleagues is, toward the end of the twentieth century, being identified in business circles with increasing frequency. In addition, public and private corporations, as well as government agencies and citizen-run enterprises, are speaking increasingly of the need to pay more attention to the development of cadres of articulate executive officers, middle-level managers, and supervisors. Automation and new thinking about the philosophical approaches to and psychological effects of work have brought changes that mean that creative decision-making and communication skills, and the understanding that must go with these, will be basic requirements for the general citizenry in the next decade. Thus, basic skills as the separable, quantifiable, isolated proficiencies that have been traditionally revered in schooling are no longer basic in the work force.

The hope—if not the promise—of the kinds of activities of the students and teachers described here is the development of problem-solving and communication skills for learners working together to display their expertise with peers and with access to an accomplished adult. But in order to realize this promise, as language learners and as teachers and researchers, we must reconsider the positions we may have taken previously on five issues central to building investments in the future of all students, especially the language-minority learners who are now regarded as being at risk.

1. We have accepted the *direction of the learning process* for all children as linear and progressive. Yet, we know from our own experience—and abundantly from the theoretical literature on language learning—that the directions of language learning are curvilinear and cyclical, and even sometimes regressive, turning back on themselves and spiraling out again. (How many times do all language learners learn to spell a word or handle a grammar problem in a foreign language, only to lose it again in a month?)
2. We have expected the *rate of learning* to be incremental, rather than characterized by quantum transformations and periods of latency. Yet, we know from our own conscious learning that it moves in spurts that are determined largely by our own intentional control over what we want to know and when we need to know.

49

3. We have limited the *agents and settings of language learning* to teachers and schools, with only occasional nods toward parents and homes. We have done relatively little to collaborate with volunteer institutions—such as Boy and Girl Scouts and church groups—which often support and promote the habits of self-discipline and teamwork endorsed by the school. We have, on the one hand, assumed the educational establishment's control over students' learning, while acknowledging, on the other hand, the necessity of learning as a lifelong experience.

4. We have placed the *substance of teaching* in technical and commercial artifacts—textbooks, workbooks, and laboratories—instead of human interactions. Isolated as teachers, we have cut ourselves off from the readiest of learning resources—our students and their communicative worlds beyond their hours at school.

5. We have melded *sociocultural identities* into sameness. Finding ourselves fearful of the magnificent diversity in which human potentials are realized in sociocultural communities, we have not allowed ourselves to bring the full range of language habits of which human speech communities are capable into the classroom as texts, as sources of data to inform us of the multiple ways in which we can use language to accomplish social goals. To avoid considering the taboo issues of race, culture, gender difference, and varying life styles, we have too often cited poverty as the critical factor in life chances and life choices.

To build on the riches of diverse language forms and uses depends on relinquishing our previously held positions. The basic stuff of human learning—behaviors, motivations, and intentions—cannot be "standardized" or measured, for psychological, social, and cultural "laws" shed their predictability with altered contexts. Hence, attempts to reduce language learning, or any learning, to strategies imitative of mechanical patterns of progress prevent society from investing in its youth. Human well-being and security in the coming decades will turn on the capacity of teachers, researchers, and students to overcome and resist rulelike and conventionalized views of education and of their separate roles. They must invent and accomplish collaborative, theoretically generative, and reflective versions of learning. Language, by virtue of its central place in knowledge transmission and transformation, stands as the first candidate for this compelling obligation.

APPENDIXES

A. IMPLEMENTING CROSS-GRADE TUTORING PROJECTS

The suggestions below summarize important lessons about implementing cross-grade tutoring projects learned by educators working in several such projects in different types of schools in the United States.

1. Allow a preparation period of at least one month to six weeks for the student tutors. During this time, tutors come to understand the focus on literate behaviors. They also learn about the tutoring process itself and have an opportunity to familiarize themselves with the books that they will read to their tutees.

2. Use as much writing as possible in the context of the tutoring from the very beginning. Include letters, book translations, book reviews, scripts adapted from books (so that children can do mini-plays), etc. Try to give the tutors every possible opportunity to use their tutoring experience as a basis for writing to different audiences—including their tutees. Such writing could include letters, written conversations worked out together, stories or books for the tutees, texts for picture books, and transcriptions of stories told by the tutees.

3. Make field notes meaningful as a basis for conversation by providing students with occasions to share their notes orally. Students need opportunities to talk about their field notes. One such way is to have students share their notes during small-group tutor conferences. Approximately fifteen minutes of time for writing field notes after each tutoring session is sufficient for generating as much as a half-hour of intense discussion among tutors.

4. Provide students with supportive models of open-ended questioning. Talk about the emptiness of questions that can

be answered with only *yes* or *no*. Encourage students to think of all the different ways that we ask questions and to try to use each of the ways they have listed at least once in each tutoring session.

5. Emphasize the ways in which tutors can extend tutees' responses and elicit elaboration from tutees in order to impress upon them the importance of talk in learning. Tutors commonly ignore tutees' comments or simply say "uh huh" and thus miss a valuable occasion for elaboration. Writing conferences between a tutor and a tutee can provide time for students to discuss tutees' reactions and learn patterns of elaboration and elicitation.

6. Discuss the ways the book's content relates to students' experiences. Extend reading sessions beyond the time it actually takes to read the book. Discussion of the book should begin before reading and continue after the reading has been completed. Tutors should know several ways to continue discussion or pursue other followup activities after completing the reading of a book or story.

7. Provide opportunities for tutors to prepare their reading. They should have a chance to preread the books and plan some questions or writing activities before they read with their tutees.

8. Develop real audiences for students' written work. For example, students could write to other classes, other schools, parents, or future tutors. Remember the fifth and sixth graders in Texas who wrote a book for parents of kindergartners in which they expressed their ideas about tutoring and how important it is for parents to read to young children.

9. View the tutoring experience as academic language study. Reading, writing about and discussing reading, describing events, analyzing relationships, and drawing conclusions form the fundamental core of academic demands in the higher grades.

What are some questions often raised about cross-grade tutoring? Aside from organizational difficulties, this practice raises some questions that are of concern to both researchers and teachers.

Question: Are we doing younger students a disservice by having them tutored by older students who may not be of the same language and culture group or who may not be at the top of their classes in reading and writing? In other words, might not some students' literate development be impaired by having less than perfect academic and Standard English models?

Answer: An essential part of any cross-grade tutoring program is training the older students to act as competent tutors, no matter what their reading/writing level. Research on collaborative learning has shown that though medium and low achievers benefit more from such learning than high achievers do, such benefit is not bought at the expense of high achievers, who perform equally well in both learning environments. All would-be tutors need to be given instruction in tutoring through modeling, watching videotapes, and discussing the activity and its meaning with teachers and other tutors. Most importantly, tutors must understand that they have a responsibility for their tutees' learning as well as their own. This responsibility goes beyond simply reading to the younger students to include accounting for the tutees' reactions and progress. The tutors must be made aware of what is expected of them as readers, writers, reporters—and, above all, models—during their participation. If tutors are educated to see themselves as responsible and competent models for their tutees, the younger students always benefit.

Question: Do older students (tutors) get something out of tutoring that they do not obtain from "traditional" direct instruction?

Answer: Clearly students need both direct instruction and experience as tutors. Research on various forms of collaborative learning tends to show that in the three areas deemed important for the school instruction of minority students—school achievement, creation of positive race relations, and socialization toward social values—cooperative learning almost always shows more positive results than traditional learning does. Both mainstream and minority students show far greater increases in academic achievement when they participate in collaborative learning projects than when they remain in traditional teacher-focused classrooms. We should note that many advanced placement and honors classes focus on collaborative learning with the view that thorough content-based learning depends on sharing knowledge through talking and writing.

Question: Given the fact that today's schools already demand so much of teachers, is it desirable or even possible to burden teachers with yet one more responsibility?

Answer: It is certainly true that teachers in today's schools are faced with almost overwhelming demands on their time and energy, particularly when they begin to implement various innovations in educational practice in their classrooms. With projects such as cross-grade tutoring in reading and writing, however, teachers' involvement is crucial. By acting as literate models for students, teachers also model behaviors that can be used by students in their own homes—for example, in helping siblings with homework. The promise that such forms of learning have for dealing with important and pressing issues in the education of minority students should not—and, indeed, cannot—be ignored, for it is when teachers can integrate learning outside the school with what happens inside the classroom that minority students move to academic competence.

Question: How can the growth of literate behaviors through cross-grade tutoring be documented? Are such projects worth the effort and energy?

Answer: It is without a doubt much more difficult to assess the outcomes of cross-grade tutoring than it is to evaluate more traditional teacher-centered instruction. The fact that such projects require the long-term commitment and involvement of both students and teachers makes the task of assessment difficult since "results" may not appear over the short term. Furthermore, just which changes should be regarded as significant—as well as just which ways should be used to measure them—poses important problems. Yet, many agree that the traditional ways of assessing students' learning—ascertaining whether students can get the "right answers" to close-ended questions—do not adequately account for students' language competence. If teachers can supplement these tests by observing and interacting with their students during tutoring and writing sessions, they can provide profiles of changed literate behaviors in reading, talking, writing, and taking responsibility for learning. Moreover, the writing that students do over the course of the program will show definite changes that the students themselves can assess and describe in their own profiles.

B. REFERENCES AND SUGGESTED READINGS

Atwell, Nancie. *In the Middle: Writing, Reading, and Learning with Adolescents.* Portsmouth, N.H.: Boynton/Cook, 1987.

This book is written by a teacher whose respect for her students and their differences shines through every story she tells and each activity she recommends. She workshops with her students as they read and write; she has mini-lessons on everything from grammatical minutiae to poetry and historical orations. Her evidence should convince even the most resistant educators of the power of connecting reading to writing and of letting students learn grammar through using language in a range of genres for many audiences. Though her focus is on middle school students, the methods she illustrates apply to students of all ages.

Au, Kathryn Hu-Pei, and Cathie Jordan. "Teaching Reading to Hawaiian Children: Finding a Culturally Appropriate Solution." In *Culture and the Bilingual Classroom: Studies in Classroom Ethnography,* edited by H. T. Trueba, G. P. Guthrie, and K. H. Au. Rowley, Mass.: Newbury House, 1981.

This article describes the Kamehameha Early Education Program (KEEP), an experimental school where teachers and researchers worked together to improve the early schooling experiences of urban Hawaiian children who typically have faced school failure. The authors tell how successful reading instruction was achieved by replicating in the classroom the ways in which language was used in the community. The article illustrates how educators can foster learning by developing classroom activities that are congruent with the children's home and community experiences.

Bilingual Education Office, California State Department of Education. *Beyond Language: Social and Cultural Factors in Schooling Language Minority Students.* Los Angeles: California State University, Evaluation, Dissemination, and Assessment Center, 1986.

This collection of articles speaks directly to educators about ways that language habits connect with the social and cultural features of the lives of language-minority students. Several chapters compare language uses in school with those in language minority communities and suggest practical classroom and district policies. The authors illustrate ways that students learn together in classroom activities as well as in community contexts linked to the school through the combined efforts of researchers and teachers.

Cummins, Jim. "The Role of Primary Language Development in Promoting Educational Success for Language Minority Students. In *Schooling and Language Minority Students: A Theoretical Framework,* edited by Office of Bilingual Bicultural Education, California State Department of Education. Los Angeles: California State University, Evaluation, Dissemination, and Assessment Center, 1981.

In this article Cummins argues that while linguistic-minority students learn very quickly how to communicate in face-to-face interactions, they take much longer to learn the sorts of academic and cognitive language abilities needed to compete in school. He believes that the linguistic-minority student's poor school performance is wrongly attributed to academic deficits in the child, rather than imperfect mastery of the language. Cummins also proposes useful theories to explain how literacy development fits with second language acquisition in school contexts.

Edelsky, Carole. *Writing in a Bilingual Program: Había una vez.* Norwood, N.J.: Ablex, 1986.

In this book the writing development of primary school children enrolled in a Spanish-English bilingual program is examined. The book, part of which is dedicated to debunking prominent "myths" about second-language learning and literacy skills—for example, that children confuse L1 and L2 writing systems—gives readers a new perspective on the rich linguistic and cultural knowledge that language-minority children bring with them to writing tasks. The evolution of the children's writing is contextualized in terms of the influence of teachers, school district politics, and community goals.

Floden, Robert E., Margaret Buchmann, and John R. Schwille. "Breaking with Everyday Experience." *Teachers College Record* 88 no. 4 (1987): 485–506.

This article cuts to the heart of the central issue in schooling for language-minority children: To what extent and in which ways should the school break with or derive content from their everyday lives? The authors argue that no institution except the school currently takes responsibility for presenting students with a range of options for living and thinking. Thus, it is within school that all students should meet diverse experiences, disciplinary concepts, and new, expanded ways of describing and assessing experience. There is much in this article that merits lively discussions among educators.

Goswami, Dixie, and Peter R. Stillman, eds. *Reclaiming the Classroom: Teacher Research as an Agency for Change.* Upper Montclair, N.J.: Boynton/Cook, 1987.

This collection of articles written by teachers and teacher advocates begins with this warning: "the hardest bit is making the familiar classroom strange to yourself." Several writers tell how they shed habits of standing at the front of the classroom and talking all the time to take up new ways of looking and learning with students. Several "big names" in language research reflect on how they came to be advocates of practices and theories that would recognize teachers as professional learners.

Graves, Donald H. *Writing: Teachers and Students at Work.* Portsmouth, N.H.: Heinemann, 1983.

This book elegantly combines research perspectives on students' writing development with insights and vignettes from classroom practice. It provides both a rationale for and practical guide to helping students take control of their own writing. The book will also assist teachers who wish to take on the roles of writing colleague and facilitator. Also, Graves provides a compelling argument for the integration of reading and writing instruction. Although not specifically focused on language-minority students, Graves' approach is quite compatible with the ideals expressed in this monograph.

Hakuta, Kenji. *Mirror of Language: The Debate on Bilingualism.* New York: Basic Books, 1986.

This very readable book contextualizes the current debates over bilingualism and bilingual education in terms of scholarly thought. Hakuta reviews research on such topics as bilingualism and intelligence, second-language learning by children and adults, and the role of bilingualism in school and society. The discussions provide an invaluable background for educators of linguistic-minority students and strong arguments for advocates of bilingual education.

Heath, Shirley Brice, and Amanda Branscombe. "Intelligent Writing in an Audience Community: Teacher, Students, and Researcher." In *The Acquisition of Written Language: Response and Revision,* edited by Sarah Warshauer Freedman. Norwood, N.J.: Ablex, 1985.

This article demonstrates how a teacher of special-education minority students worked with a researcher to involve these students in studying their own language uses. Two case studies of students' writings over the course of a year illustrate the types of changes that came for the students through participation in a variety of types of fieldwork, data analysis, and oral and written reporting of results.

Lightfoot, Martin, and Nancy Martin, eds. *The Word for Teaching Is Learning: Essays for James Britton.* London: Heinemann, 1988.

The voices of language-minority students come through in numerous chapters of this book. Teachers focus on mother-tongue instruction, literacy, and coming to terms with the world as they illustrate how their practices fed their theories of learning and how their examinations of student learning informed and reformed both theories and practices. Children's drawings and stories receive considerable attention in the book from teachers who find them useful for understanding issues of control and intention for children.

Moll, Luis, and Rosa Diaz. "Teaching Writing as Communication: The Use of Ethnographic Findings in Classroom Practice." In *Literacy and Schooling,* edited by D. Bloome. Norwood, N.J.: Ablex, 1987.

Drawing on the work of L. S. Vygotsky, a Russian psychologist, Moll and Diaz assert that learning occurs when children must stretch their capabilities within reason, working at a level where more proficient individuals assist them in accomplishing tasks, rather than at a level where they are already capable of independent mastery. The authors describe a project in which researchers and teachers formed a team to bring home and community uses of language into the school and to use Vygotskian ideas to shape classroom instruction.

Philips, Susan U. "Participant Structures and Communicative Competence: Warm Springs Children in Community and Classroom." In *Functions of Language in the Classroom,* edited by C. B. Cazden, V. P. John, and D. Hymes. Prospect Heights, Ill.: Waveland Press, 1972.

In this article Philips describes the ways in which the verbal and nonverbal communication of Native American children caused conflicts and misunderstandings when they interacted with Anglo teachers who had different unconscious norms for interaction. These conflicts, in turn, made it difficult for the children to respond to classroom expectations. This compelling story has important implications for educators working with children whose linguistic and cultural backgrounds are different from their own.

THE AUTHORS

Shirley Brice Heath began her teaching career in bilingual classrooms in southern California, and she has taught in classrooms of language-minority students in several states. Her interest in sociopolitical and cultural influences on language learning led to a doctoral degree in anthropology and linguistics from Columbia University. Her first book, *Telling Tongues: Language Policy in Mexico, Colony to Nation* (1972), traced the history of policies toward indigenous languages in Mexico. She later returned to the United States to study patterns of language learning in the schools and communities of children from Black and white working-class families in the southeastern United States. She documented this work, as well as her collaboration with teachers, in *Ways with Words: Language, Life, and Work in Communities and Classrooms* (1983). She collaborates extensively with teachers and students in classrooms of language-minority students, several of whom have been her co-authors.

Leslie Mangiola began her teaching career as an assistant teacher during her senior year at Antioch College in Ohio. She saw there the model of teaching she wanted to follow—one of collaborating to learn with students. But she had to wait twenty years (including a long hiatus to bring up four children) before she could rediscover a supportive environment for collaborating with students. She found it in Fair Oaks Elementary School in Redwood City, California, a bilingual whole-language school, where she has spent the past ten years. She has team-taught numerous workshops in northern California and has authored a chapter about her experiences with cross-grade interactive tutoring in *Becoming a Whole Language School* (1989).

THE NEA/AERA NATIONAL ADVISORY PANEL

Chair:

Sarah Warshauer Freedman, University of California, Berkeley

AERA Representatives:

Richard Duran, University of California, Santa Barbara

Robert Gundlach, Northwestern University, Evanston, Illinois

Julie Jensen, University of Texas, Austin

Martha King, Ohio State University, Columbus

Mike Rose, University of California, Los Angeles

Nancy Spivey, Carnegie Mellon University, Pittsburgh, Pennsylvania

NEA Representatives:

Patricia Candal, Beck Middle School, Georgetown, South Carolina

Susan M. Jackson, Reading Department, Arizona State University, Tempe

Jimmie Nations, Westwood School, Dalton, Georgia

Claire Pelton, San Jose Unified School District, California

Peggy Swoger, Mountain Brook Junior High School, Alabama

Ex-Officio Representatives:

Marcella Dianda, Program Development Specialist, NEA Instruction and Professional Development, Washington, D.C.

Glynda A. Hull, Chair, AERA Writing Special Interest Group, Berkeley, California

Sandra R. Schecter, Associate Director, Center for the Study of Writing and Literacy at Berkeley and Carnegie Mellon